The Coming Revival
Rodney M. Howard-Browne

RHBEA Publications

P.O. Box 197161, Louisville, KY 40259-7161 U.S.A.

P.O. Box 3900, Randburg 2125 South Africa

Unless otherwise indicated, all scriptural references are from the *King James Version* of the Bible.

The Coming Revival
ISBN 0-9583066-5-6
Copyright © 1991 by Rodney M. Howard-Browne

Third Printing, May 1993

Published by RHBEA Publications
P.O. Box 197161, Louisville, KY 40259-7161 U.S.A.
P.O. Box 3900, Randburg 2125 South Africa

Printed in the United States of America.

All rights reserved under International Copyright Law. Contents and/or cover may not be reproduced in whole or in part in any form without the express written consent of the publisher.

Chapter 1
Revival Begins in Your Heart

For thus saith the Lord of hosts; Yet once, it is a little while, and I will shake the heavens, and the earth, and the sea, and the dry land;

And I will shake all nations, and the desire of all nations shall come: and I will fill this house with glory, saith the Lord of hosts.

The silver is mine, and the gold is mine, saith the Lord of hosts.

The glory of this latter house shall be greater than of the former, saith the Lord of hosts: and in this place will I give peace, saith the Lord of hosts.

Haggai 2:6-9

I was looking through my archives at home, and I found several prophecies people have given concerning the coming revival.

Prophecy is for edification, exhortation, and comfort. I believe that recalling these prophecies will be a blessing to you. They pertain to this message. Prophecy always confirms what God does.

God said He does nothing without first revealing it to His prophets (Amos 3:7). The Bible also says, "...in the mouth of two or three witnesses every word may be established" (Matthew 18:16).

Before he went to be with the Lord, Smith Wigglesworth was permitted to look briefly into the end times. He caught a glimpse of the greatest revival the world has ever seen, but he told Lester Sumrall he knew he would not live to see it himself.

In 1980, the Spirit of God said through Rev. Kenneth E. Hagin, a prophet in the United States, that the world is on the verge of a great move and manifestation of the Spirit of God — the greatest hour in the history of the world.

When God repeats something several times, we'd better take note of it! God was saying something to us in 1980. This is eleven years later, and we're even closer to the brink of the greatest outpouring of the Spirit of God that this planet has ever seen. We saw in Haggai that the glory of the *latter* house will be *greater* than that of the former.

The Cause of Revival

Revival and its cause has been studied and discussed for years by many different people, but *revival simply begins in your heart*. Revival does not begin in your spouse's heart; it begins in you. And until revival begins in you, it's never going to begin in someone else.

You cannot experience revival if you are spiritually dead. Some Christians are as cold as a corpse. When they walk into the room, the spiritual temperature drops ten degrees, because they're part of "the frozen chosen."

If you're on fire for God and you're full of the Holy Spirit, you can take the power of God wherever you go. But too many Christians are allowing the influence of the world to stop them or pull them down.

We are the salt of the earth. We must rise up in victory, power, and faith in these last days. Then we will affect the spiritual temperature wherever we go.

Again, revival begins in your heart. Ezekiel said:

> A new heart also will I give you, and a new spirit will I put within you: and I will take away the stony heart out of your flesh, and I will give you an heart of flesh.
>
> And I will put my spirit within you....
>
> Ezekiel 36:26,27

Some people need a new spirit; that is, the Spirit of God needs to revive them. They sit like a bump on a log in the Sunday morning service, jumping up between yawns to shout "Amen!"

Revival brings a change of heart. When you have been revived, you will go and change other people's hearts — not their heads. God doesn't want fat heads; He wants fat hearts. There are enough fat heads going around! Just to change your mind is not enough; you've got to have a change of heart. That's what happens when you get born again: You have a change of heart.

Some of you are not experiencing revival right now because you need a change of heart. If you will let the Spirit of God move in your life, He will give you a change of heart, and you will be in revival. Then people will look at you and say, "Everyone's talking about revival, but that person is *walking* in it."

You can have revival all the time. You can have revival in your home. You can have revival in your car as you're commuting to work at 6 o'clock on a Monday morning. You can have revival in the midst of adverse circumstances.

Peace is not the absence of war, but the presence of God. Therefore, you can have peace in the middle of war.

When a wave of revival comes, it comes with such power that it always stirs up everything in its path. When you look inside a barrel that's filled with rain water, it looks like it contains clean water. But if you take a stick and start stirring it, you'll stir up the sediment that is on the bottom. The water that looked clean is actually dirty and full of muck!

You'll know when revival has hit, because it will affect every area of society at the same time. The Word of God is the same to the rich man as to the poor man. We're all poor without the Lord Jesus. Therefore, revival will reach out not only to the doctors and the lawyers, but also down into the gutters among the alcoholics, drunkards, prostitutes, and street people.

Chapter 2
Revival — Manifestations and the Flesh

When we mention the word "revival," Christians all over the world get nervous about "the flesh." When they see a manifestation of the flesh, they exclaim, "Oh, we saw the flesh tonight!" My reply is, "Well, you also saw the Holy Spirit."

You can't have revival without stirring up the flesh. If you want to stop the flesh, you'd better shoot everyone as they come in the door! How can you stop the flesh from manifesting in the house of God, when it is manifesting continually in the world?

"Christians" and religious people lie, cheat, backbite, and commit adultery. They are full of pride, anger, murder, debate, and so forth. The works of the flesh seen in Galatians 5 are made manifest in their lives. So what do you expect? The flesh is going to manifest.

Of course, we can stop the flesh to such a degree that no one will want to get excited. Everyone will just sit there because they're so worried about the flesh!

When revival comes, you will see manifestations

of these three things in meetings: (1) the Holy Spirit, (2) the flesh, and (3) the devil.

But I'd rather be in a church where the devil and the flesh are manifesting than in a church where nothing is happening because people are too afraid to manifest anything.

Every time there is a move of God, a few people will get excited, go overboard, and get in the flesh. The other believers will get upset, saying, "That couldn't be God." Don't worry about it. And if a devil manifests, don't worry about that, either. Rejoice, because at least *something* is happening!

Don't Quench the Spirit

You can't stop the flesh by stopping the flesh. The only way people can learn not to get in the flesh is to be taught to recognize what is of God and what is not. If you stop *every* manifestation, you will stop manifestations that *aren't* of the flesh, and thus you have stopped the Spirit of God! For example, we've seen so much of the flesh in prophecy that now many believers don't want to hear prophecy. But the Bible says, "Despise not prophesyings" (1 Thessalonians 5:20).

Don't quench the Holy Spirit. There are always enough wet blankets around to put out the fire! In the coming revival we've got to get mature enough to say, "That's the flesh. Don't worry about it."

You couldn't stir up the Spirit of God on the inside of some dear people if you tried. The only thing they're ever going to get in is the flesh! They'll leave your meeting blessed and happy in the flesh!

So instead of putting the fire out, we need to turn the heat up! When the heat is stirred up, the light will become so bright that flesh "bugs" will be attracted to it. *But they can't stay in the flesh in the presence of the anointing of God.* They may come in and turn cartwheels and do other things in the flesh, but when the anointing comes, their flesh will start getting hit, and they will have to change!

Remember, if we stop every manifestation, we will also be quenching and grieving the Spirit of God. Therefore, let's be mature enough to know what's of God and what isn't. Let's not get offended and say, "I'm not going back to that church, because the flesh or a demon manifested."

Let God Be God

Let's allow the Holy Spirit to have free rein. Let God be God. God is in control. God knows what He is doing. We might not know what we're doing, but God knows what He is doing.

Everyone has ideas about how a meeting should be run. I'd like to see some of *you* run a meeting and have a move of God. Do yourself a favor — study books on the early revivals of men like John Wesley, Charles Finney, and Peter Cartwright.

While Wesley and Cartwright preached, people fell out under the power, went into contortions, rolled on the floor, and cried out. Wesley got very bothered about it, but he finally concluded, "I'm going to let God do whatever He wants to do, however He wants to do it, and I'm not going to interfere."

If someone comes into a meeting, rolls around on the floor, laughs in the Holy Spirit, or does it in the flesh, at least he's not getting drunk or taking dope. We can help him mature in spiritual matters. Let's not criticize and judge when the Holy Spirit is moving, as we might be criticizing and judging the Holy Spirit. Let's not quench the Holy Spirit!

Chapter 3
Revivals of the Past 300 Years

As we study the revivals of the last three hundred years, we find that God moved such preachers as John Wesley, George Whitfield, and Charles Finney in awesome ways.

Finney would pray for the glory of God to saturate the whole county where he was ministering, and as soon as people drove their buggies across the county line, they would start shaking like a leaf!

The crime rate dropped dramatically in communities where he preached. Usually, bars and saloons were forced to close down for lack of business. Nearly everyone in town would get saved. People would spend hours in prayer. These were genuine outpourings of the Holy Spirit.

The powerful Welsh revival began in 1904, when a 26-year-old former miner named Evan Roberts touched his nation and the glory of God fell in answer to his agonized prayers. Intercession fell on all the Welsh Christians, and they cried out to God for the lost. As a result, more than one hundred thousand people were saved, and for two glorious years the churches of Wales were packed out.

The revival attracted international attention. Although it is not considered a Pentecostal revival, it influenced many ministers who later became Pentecostal leaders.

Today, if 10,000 people come together in a convention, we call it a "revival." It's no more a revival than a duck is a jet pilot!

I've gone to conventions where there were five speakers in one service. Five! I said, "O God!" The Lord spoke to me and said, "Son, if they'd just quit talking and let my Spirit move instead." Everyone got up and gave their two cent's worth about what they thought was going to happen. *And the moment the Holy Spirit moved, they stopped Him!* They wanted to dictate to God — but God will not be dictated to by man.

Ministers with that kind of attitude will not succeed. The day will come, even in these end times, when churches of ten to twenty thousand around the world will close their doors if they refuse to change and move with the Spirit of God.

We've found in the last twenty years in South Africa that if we will not run with the Spirit of God, God will go across town and find a church that is half dead, raise the pastor up, breathe on the congregation, and they will flow with His Spirit.

I don't want to be so full of pride, tradition, and bondage that I won't allow the Spirit of God to move.

Revival Brings Change

When revival comes, change comes. But people don't want change. "We like it this way, brother," they say. "We want our three hymns and an offertory. Just keep preaching out of the encyclopedia and the *Reader's Digest*. Then afterwards, you can put your cold hand on my fevered brow — I'd really appreciate it — but don't do anything out of the ordinary. Just keep it normal."

It's time we started having the abnormal in our services! It's time we started having something supernatural. People today talk a great deal about the Spirit of God, but if Jesus were here, they'd run away from Him! If Paul were here, they'd run away from him! If Smith Wigglesworth were here, they'd run away from him! "Too radical," they'd say.

A New Century of Revival

In January 1901, a revival was ignited in an independent Bible school run by Charles F. Parham in Topeka, Kansas. Although Parham wasn't baptized in the Holy Spirit himself, he challenged his students to study the biblical evidence of the baptism in the Holy Spirit.

On January 1, 1901, a young woman spoke in tongues. Within a few days, Parham and half the student body were also baptized in the Spirit, speaking in tongues. This revival eventually spread around the world, and today Parham is recognized as the founder of the Pentecostal Movement.

Parham moved his school to Houston in December 1905. There, a black evangelist by the name of William J. "Daddy" Seymour desperately wanted to attend the classes, but it was against the law in Texas for a black man to attend a white school. Parham followed a higher law and allowed Seymour to sit outside in the hallway.

In 1906, Seymour was invited to pastor a Holiness church in Los Angeles. Parham gave him the money for his train ticket. The group locked Seymour out of their church when he began preaching on tongues as the evidence of the Pentecostal experience — an experience he himself was still seeking.

Seymour was then invited to hold prayer meetings in a house on Bonnie Brae Avenue. There, Seymour and many others received the baptism in the Holy Spirit with tongues. Word spread quickly.

After a few weeks, crowds were gathering outside, so Seymour's group rented a run-down building on Azusa Street. It had once been a church, then a stable, and finally a warehouse. The first service was held on April 14, 1906. A month later, a thousand people were trying to squeeze into the little mission.

Its meek, one-eyed pastor didn't have a 5,000-seat church. He didn't have a great choir. He didn't have beautiful chandeliers. His "pews" were planks resting on nail kegs. But Daddy Seymour would sit praying, his head covered, behind the rough shoe boxes that were used as a pulpit. He knew how to pray heaven down and hell out the door!

Such a mighty revival visited the Azusa Street Mission in 1906 that thousands of hungry people from all races, cultures, and denominations made their way to Azusa Street from literally the ends of the earth to receive the Pentecostal experience. The initial revival lasted three years. Meetings were held three times a day seven days a week.

Different revivals continued in the twenties and thirties. When the great Healing Revival started in 1947, more great men of God were raised up, including A. A. Allen, Jack Coe, William Branham, T. L. Osborn, and Oral Roberts.

Some had huge tents, where great and mighty miracles occurred. Preachers would advertize, "The blind see, the lame walk, and the deaf hear!" And the blind *did* see, and the lame *did* walk, and the deaf *did* hear.

Today in the states, people still advertize, "The blind see, the lame walk, and the deaf hear." When you go there, you find that the deaf walk, the lame see, and the blind talk. Nothing happens! But from 1947-59, a wave of healing and miracles swept the country.

Catching the Next Wave

If a revival comes with a wave, we've got to ride that wave. If we don't, we'll end up on the beach.

A surfer doesn't ride his board all the way to the white foam on the beach; he turns, paddles back, and looks for the *next* wave. But he doesn't take just any wave; he catches the *right* wave.

There's a *right* wave and there's a *wrong* wave. You have to know how to "read" the waves. If you stay with the wrong wave, you and your board will end up smashed on the sand!

Men and women of God have ridden the right wave in the past, but they continued to ride it after the new one came. They didn't want to change. "We love this wave," they said. "This is our special wave." But it's over!

When a wave is over, look for the next wave. And when that one is over, look for the next. Don't stand on the beach, saying, "Oh, I remember that wonderful 1914 wave. It was so big, I carried three people on my surfboard. I've got photographs of it. Do you want to see them?"

The Healing Revival *was* awesome. It was followed by the Latter Rain Movement in the fifties. Then, in the sixties, we saw the Charismatic Movement break out. The power of God moved out of the Pentecostal abominations — I mean, denominations — and Methodists, Baptists, Presbyterians, Catholics, and others started getting filled with the Spirit of God and speaking in tongues.

Many Pentecostals couldn't swallow that. "*No!* It's *impossible* for a Catholic to get baptized in the Holy Spirit!" That's what they thought. But people were filled with the Holy Spirit anyway.

Aren't you grateful for that charismatic wave? We saw the Spirit of God go beyond boundaries and borders. But that wave came to an end, too.

Trapped in the Past

As I've traveled around the United States, I've visited some tent meetings. I've watched film footage from the early forties and fifties, and when I entered these modern tent meetings, I sensed that I had stepped back into the year 1951!

The choir members are dressed just like the choirs of 1951. They sing the same songs and choruses: "Jesus on the main line; tell Him what you want." They have a ramp for wheelchairs. They talk the same. They introduce the speaker the same: "God's man of faith and power." Time seems to have stopped for them forty years ago during the Healing Movement.

I've been to churches that are still living in the Charismatic Movement. Do you remember when you came to church in sandals and shorts, everyone sang scripture choruses, and people went around with a bowl and washed each other's feet and hugged everyone?

Seminars, Translations, and Tapes

In the seventies we saw the outbreak of what we call the Word of Faith or Teaching Movement. When that wave hit, the "in" thing was seminars, seminars, seminars. And Bible translations — Greek ones, Hebrew ones, whatever. And lots of Bibles — big Bibles, fat Bibles, tall Bibles — the Word, the Word, the Word.

Confess the Word. Talk the Word. Live the Word. Eat the Word. Sleep the Word. Fly the Word. You had five thousand cassette tapes on your shelf. When you staggered out of your house at 2 o'clock in the afternoon, you said, "Hallelujah, I've gone through ten tapes today. I'm in the Word! Did you make your confessions today? A confession a day will keep the devil away."

You tried to talk to people: Maybe you'd ask a simple question. "How are you doing today?"

"I'm *blessed*. Praise God, hallelujah, I'm the righteousness of God in Christ Jesus. Hallelujah, I cannot be defeated, and I will not quit. Hallelujah, I'm the head and not the tail!"

"Brother, how *are* you?"

"I'm *blessed,* brother. Praise God." But when you looked out the window, his car was being towed away!

If a man came in on crutches and you asked, "How are you," he would say, "I'm healed and whole. Hallelujah, I don't have a problem."

In some instances, you could never relate to some people!

Then the excesses came. Everyone had to have a Brand X watch and drive an XYZ car, or they didn't have the anointing. And everyone had to get in agreement with you. "Would you get in agreement with me, brother? Please be in agreement with me."

I'm not knocking this; I'm just pointing out that every move develops its own traditions. Therefore, let us not be critical of others, for in the latest move we've been very critical of others. We're just as much to blame as everyone else!

For example, when the offering comes, the people are told, "Everyone lift their hand toward the offering." They don't even know why they're doing it. Some think they are waving their money good-bye. We slip into tradition so easily.

The early Pentecostals prayed a certain way. It had to be full-blown steam, or it wasn't anointed. Today people pray a certain way: "Father God, we thank You. Father God, touch the people. And, Father God, we can all go home."

The early Pentecostals prophesied like this: "For the Lord shall say unto thee, for even thou shalt know..." You thought the earth was going to open! You thought it was doomsday!

Today the prophecy sounds like, "For, yea, thou art a blessing, and your praises are sweet before Me, saith the Lord. They're good for my health..."

Tradition — tradition — it's all tradition!

Jumping Overboard

Every move of the Spirit of God is accompanied by excesses. These excesses come because there are always people who jump overboard.

In the Healing Revival, it didn't matter if you looked like you were going to get sick next year — they'd pray for you. They would look at you and *find* something wrong with you.

Things sometimes were strange in the Charismatic Movement, too. They would want to get you filled with the Holy Spirit; *then* get you saved. "Speak in tongues. You got it, brother. Now come and get saved."

In the Teaching Wave Movement, everything was prosperity, who I am in Christ, and I'm this and I'm that. The Lord spoke to me and said that in some circles there's been too much emphasis on who and what we are and not on who and what He is. It brought a lot of arrogance into the Body of Christ. You couldn't mix with anyone if they could taint you.

If someone came with a *problem*, people got upset. "Oh, brother, don't bring that around *here!* That's *negative* and I'm positive. Don't bring negative things around here."

Well, obviously you can't be too positive if you're worried about something negative. You must deal with people's problems. If you can't listen to what they've got to say, and you can't help them out of their problems, there's something wrong with you and with what you believe.

Fresh Bread

I believe that this teaching revival as it was in the '70s and '80s came to an end. Some men of God are still teaching things that we heard fifteen years ago. That's not completely wrong, for we all must hear the basics — but surely God is saying something fresh in the earth today.

I don't want stale bread. You should know by now that you're the righteousness of God in Christ Jesus. If you don't, you'd better take some elementary training and learn how to become the righteousness of God.

God is saying a new thing. Yes, everything in the Word is true, but there's a fresh anointing. There's an excitement. There's a joy. *There are things pertaining to this hour of history that God wants to speak to the Church.*

I've gone to some churches in the states where the speaker got up and said, "Today I want to talk about twenty ways to become prosperous and get a new car."

I thought, "God, have mercy! We're through with all that junk. Who cares what kind of car you drive? God doesn't care what car you drive."

People get so hung up about the way you live, how you dress, and what you drive. They're missing the whole importance of why we're here on earth. Who cares where you live? If you're happy living there, go ahead and live there. If you've got three bedrooms and horses live in two of them, that's your business.

We become hung up on material things that are non-essential to eternal life. When you get to heaven, is God going to say, "Well done, thou good and *successful* servant. Bring that fancy wristwatch here. I've always wanted one myself, to be honest with you."

No! He's going to say, "Well done, thou good and *faithful* servant."

Chapter 4
What the Coming Revival Will Be

Those who understand the movings of the Holy Spirit and can read the signs know that things began to change about 1982-83. What's been happening since 1983? There has been a time of preparation; a time of cleansing. Things that were not right have been judged.

God is dealing with the people and their leaders. Those who won't humble themselves will be humbled: God will pull the rug out from under them!

God is getting us all to the place where we are nothing and He is everything. God is burning, by the Holy Spirit, all the rubbish out of us and is making us vessels of honor, sanctified and meet for the Master's use. Why? For the coming revival.

There will be no great men in the coming revival. There will be no great women in the coming revival. There will be ordinary men and ordinary women with a great God.

They will rise up and tell the story of the cross. They will take this Gospel to the ends of the earth. I tell you by the Spirit of God that there are people who have been sitting in churches for ten, fifteen, and twenty years who never thought God would ever use them in the ministry — but in this final outpouring of the Holy Spirit, God will breathe upon them, and in one moment of time they shall have a visitation from the Lord.

People will even sell their houses and their businesses, and they shall go to foreign fields. For the time is short, and God shall raise up this army of men and women. Do not say, "I am not useful." But say, "God, use me. You're my God. Send me."

God seeks a people who are willing. God seeks a people who are yielded. God seeks a people who will count the cost. God seeks a people who will lend their lives unto Him, and He shall flow through them and touch many.

This is the day and the hour of the outpouring of the Spirit of God. This is the day, the final moment, of the Church. It's time to get ready. Don't sit back and say, "God's not going to use me." Start getting yourself ready.

I'm convinced in my heart that within five years from today, if Jesus tarries, some of you who never, ever thought that you were called — everyone around you didn't think you were called, either — will walk into your living room one day and suddenly an angel will appear to you.

And God will burn things out of you, and you'll sell your business, and you'll sell your house and your belongings, and you'll leave. You'll obey the call of God. God is going to do it.

This is not necessarily going to happen to people who have been through Bible school. A diploma can't heal anyone. Place your doctorate on a wheelchair patient in the Name of Jesus, and see what happens.

The devil's not afraid of a diploma. When you show him that piece of paper, he'll pull out his diploma and say, "Join the gang — you and I went to the same school!" The power of God is not going to flow through those who have theory; it's going to flow through those who have revelation.

Does that mean I don't believe in teaching? No, we must have teaching, and teaching will be a part of the move of the nineties.

Demonstrating the Power of God

The move of God in the nineties will not just be teaching alone. We must demonstrate. The time has come to demonstrate the power of God!

You've heard how to lay hands on the sick — now do it!

You've heard how to cast out devils — now do it!

You've heard how to operate in the gifts — now do it!

Do it!

Prophesy, some of you. Stir yourselves up in the Holy Spirit. Start doing it in your workplace. Don't wait. Start making yourself available to meet the needs around you. Go to the man in the street. Go to your next-door neighbor. Get on the telephone. Get excited about the things of God. When the move comes, people will be excited!

Don't just go to church. Take the unsaved with you. Take the sick with you. Take the needy with you. Go expecting God to move. Stir yourself up!

I believe we slipped over the edge into this great outpouring in 1990.

As the prophets old and new have said, we're on the edge, the brink, of the coming revival. I can see the dark clouds on the horizon. I can hear the distant thunder. I can see the flashes of lightning.

The first drops of rain are beginning to fall from the final wave of God's glory!

The Coming Revival

The coming revival will be a culmination of all other revivals. There will be teaching, preaching, signs and wonders, healings, miracles, the glory of God, people being translated by the Spirit as Philip was in the Book of Acts, and people being raised from the dead.

There will be awesome manifestations of the glory of God. Creative miracles will happen: Eyeballs will form, legs and arms will grow out, people will leap out of wheelchairs.

God will use people everywhere — from all walks of life and all denominations — and the coming revival will not be limited to just one group. It will include the whole Body of Christ.

God is preparing His Church. There will never be one group of people who will be able to say, "We're the ones who are heading up this revival."

Revival will cover the earth! People will shout, "Come over to this side of town. Come and see the move of God!" The other Christians will say, "It's over here in our church, too!"

People will say, "Come to America," because there will be a great revival in America. You in foreign countries will be able to say, "We don't need to go to America; the revival's here!" The glory of the Lord will cover the earth as the water covers the sea.

No man will control this move of God. If we won't receive it, God will go to another place and raise up a people there. Revival will spread into the highways and the byways.

The Final Harvest

The greatest harvest of the lost will occur in these last days. There will be nothing that ever happened before that we can measure it by. People will knock on your door at night and say, "An angel met me in the street and said, 'Go in there.'"

We will see supernatural manifestations. There will be times in services when angels will be seen. No one will have to wonder if this is the Spirit or the flesh. When a ten-foot angel stands in front of you, you'll repent and get saved! One look at him will scare the devil out of you!

There will be a revival in the local churches. Local churches are going to spring up everywhere. I did a study on the top hundred cities in the United States. To get the job done, every large city needs ten more churches of 10,000 people each, because when the last harvest comes, there will not be enough churches to accommodate the crowds!

When the final revival comes, you will probably use your average-sized church as a place to serve refreshments, because it won't be large enough for services.

The glory of God will sweep everywhere. We will pack stadiums and football fields. The coming revival will shake cities, towns, and villages.

Revival Brings Judgment

With this revival, the judgment of God will start to fall. Judgment will come on nations, on cities, and on people that oppose that which God will do in these last days, for the will of God will be accomplished — the plan of God will come to pass. When God works a work, no man can stop it. When God stops a work, no man can work it. God will deal with people who mock the Spirit of God or the move of God.

One of these days a true prophet, anointed of God, will be a guest on one of these television talk shows. When they start to mock him, he will simply look at them and say, "That you may know that there is a God who lives — that you may know that He shall not be mocked — you will be blind for three days as a sign to you and this audience."

The talk show host will scream, "O my God, I can't see! I can't see! I'm blind!" And the telephone lines will be jammed; signs and wonders will be made manifest.

Hidden Sins Will Be Revealed

We will start seeing people drop dead when they lie about hidden sin, like Ananias and Sapphira did. Sinful, evil men will drop dead in their pulpits. It will be as it was in the Book of Acts: A great fear will come upon the whole Church.

You don't have anything to worry about if you have repented of your sins and your heart is right with God. But if you are a two-faced liar, full of the devil, and you want to be a part of this move of God, you will be exposed.

There will come a sorting out. We will know who the sheep are and who the goats are. Everything that is hidden, and all lying, cheating, and backbiting, will be revealed.

And when we all stand before God naked, with nothing, we will know it's not by works of righteousness which we have done, but by the blood of Jesus and by His power and grace.

There will be an explosion of the power of the Holy Spirit, much like there was on the Day of Pentecost, when they were all together in one accord, and suddenly there came a sound from heaven. We're on the brink of it right now. *Suddenly,* it's going to come!

We are moving into the final outpouring of God's supernatural power. His power will fill villages, towns, cities, states, and provinces. Whole nations will be changed. Get ready! This is not the time to quit. We must reap the harvest.

You ask, "What will happen next?" We will experience the greatest revival in history for four or five years. *We will also experience intense persecution which will cost some people their lives.* **We are living in perilous times!**

Then Jesus Christ will split the eastern sky. "The dead in Christ shall rise first: Then we which are alive and remain will be caught up together with them in the air: and so shall we ever be with the Lord"! (1 Thessalonians 4:16,17).

Sermon Outline:
The Coming Revival

Foundation Scripture — Haggai 2:6-9

1. *Revival begins in your heart*
    a. Ezekiel 36:26,27
    b. Revival brings a change of heart
    c. Revival will stir you up — on fire for God — will affect every area of society
2. *Revival — manifestations and the flesh*
    a. Spirit, soul, and body
    b. Demons — flesh — spirit (3 manifestations)
    c. If we stop everything, we will quench and grieve the Holy Spirit
    d. Signs and wonders
3. *Revivals of the past 300 years*
    a. John Wesley, George Whitfield, Charles Finney, Peter Cartwright
    b. 1904 Welsh Revival — Evan Roberts, 26 years old
    c. 1901 — Topeka, Kansas — Charles F. Parham
    d. 1906 — Azusa Street — William J. "Daddy" Seymour
    e. 1947-59 — Healing Revival — many leaders

f. 1960-70 — Charismatic Revival — many leaders
   g. 1970-80 — Teaching (Word) Revival — many leaders
   h. 1983-90 — Great Change
   i. 1990s (The Decade of the '90s) — Great Outpouring
4. *The coming revival will be*
   a. A revival — which is a combination of all that has happened from Acts until now — not just one group or denomination — local churches raised up — villages, towns, states, even whole nations, shaken
   b. Explosion of Holy Spirit power like the Day of Pentecost — greater — signs and wonders, judgment and persecution
   c. The glory of the Lord will be seen

For information regarding books, audio tapes, and videotapes, please write us at Rodney Howard-Browne Evangelistic Association at one of the addresses listed below:

RHBEA Publications
P.O. Box 197161, Louisville, KY 40259-7161 U.S.A.
P.O. Box 3900, Randburg 2125 South Africa